The Adventures of Toby and Dr. David

Toby's Story

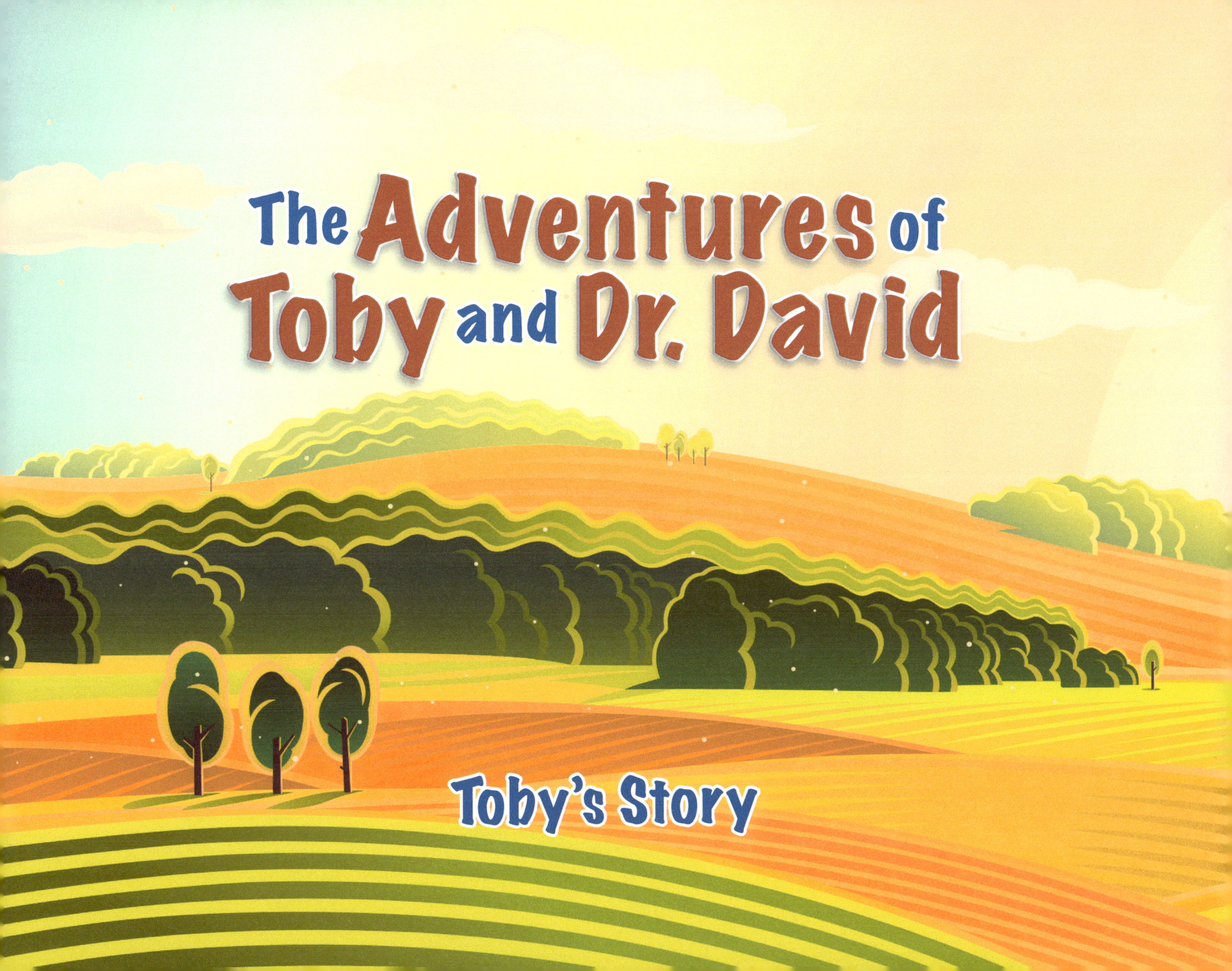

Copyright © 2018 by Chris Harbach, Beverly Behrends
All rights reserved. No part of this book may be used or reproduced in any manner whatsoever without the written permission of the author.

Author: Chris Harbach   Artist: Beverly Behrends

The Adventures of Toby and Dr. David
Toby's Story
ISBN 978-1-941516-41-6 paperback
ISBN 978-1-941516-43-0 hardback
ISBN 978-1-941516-44-7 ebook
Library of Congress Control Number: 2018958967
Educational Children's Book

Published by Franklin Scribes Publishers.
Franklin Scribes is a registered trademark of Franklin Scribes Publishers.
franklinscribeswrites@gmail.com   www.franklinscribes.com

Contact the author at
www.franklinscribes.com/chris-harbach/
Facebook page for Toby: Toby and Dr David
Website: Tobyanddrdavid.com   *Email:* admin@Tobyanddrdavid.com
Toby's Productions LLC
Front and back book covers designed by Thompson Printing Solutions
This book was printed in the United States of America.

FRANKLIN
SCRIBES™
PUBLISHERS

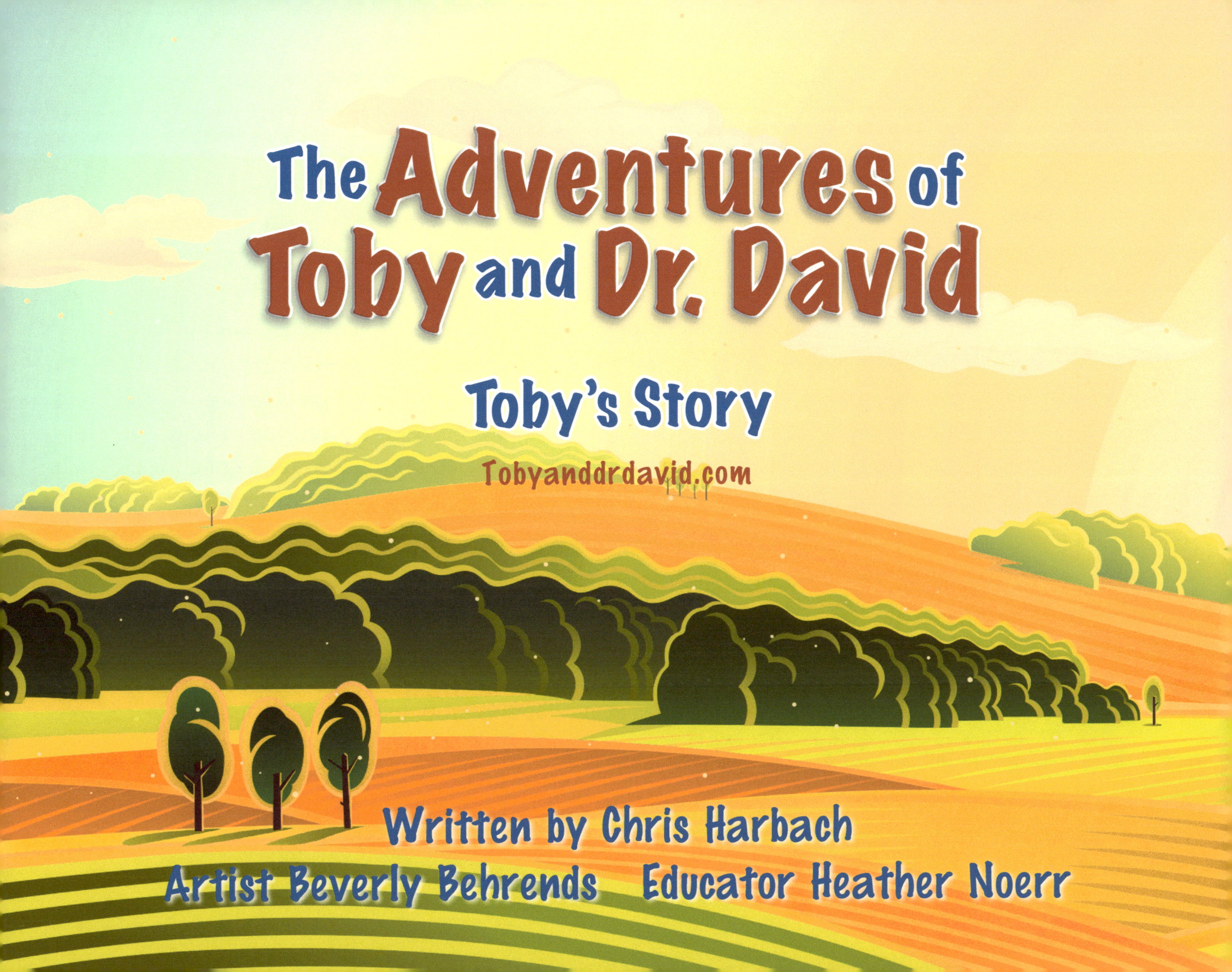

The Adventures of Toby and Dr. David

Toby's Story

Tobyanddrdavid.com

Written by Chris Harbach

Artist Beverly Behrends   Educator Heather Noerr

The Adventures of Toby and Dr. David
Toby's Story

INTRODUCTION

The Blanco Veterinary Clinic is located in Blanco, a small town in the Texas Hill Country smack dab in the middle between Austin and San Antonio. A visitor to Blanco might feel as though he has traveled a hundred years back in time, back to the hot and dusty roads and streets of the old west, back to the tough times that called for strong and courageous people and animals.

The Veterinary Clinic is owned and operated by Dr David Behrends, known to his clients and patients alike as, Dr. David. The doctor's clientele includes most every rancher and pet owner inhabiting the township and immediate outskirts of Blanco. His clinic serves all animals in the area whether they be wild, rescued or owned outright. And that animal population is some population indeed. It encompasses, every domesticated, wild, and/or exotic critter, bird and beast indigenous or otherwise imported to the South Texas ranch land. The Doctor and his clinic are very unique in this respect. The knowledge and capabilities applied and practiced extend far beyond those of most American vet clinics.

If you want to know the idiosyncrasies of every breed of cow in the area, just ask Dr. David. Better yet, if you want to learn how to handle an ostrich or a rhino, go on a farm call with him. Should you be interested in the distance he'll go to save the life of a rescue, come observe him in his operating room at the clinic. If you just want to meet all of his animal friends along with some of the more eccentric Blanco locals, heed his booming South Texas call of "Ya'ller welcome" and stop in for a visit.

The animal stories from the Blanco Vet Clinic are told by Dr. David's Labrador Retriever, Toby. Toby, a rescue dog himself, begins the series with his own story and account of the perils he faced and endured along the path he traveled to find his "forever" home with the doctor. Toby is a permanent fixture at the Blanco Vet Clinic along with the counter cat, Peetie. Weather permitting, Toby accompanies Dr. David on every farm call made weekday or weekend, day or night.

Along the way, Toby has made friendships and acquaintances with lots of animals every one of whom has its own tale of handling, rescue and treatment by Dr. David. Most owe Dr. David their life.

From Toby

 with Love

My name is Toby

I am a very lucky dog!

When I was young I would play with my brothers and sisters every day.

Pretty soon we were given away.
I had a new friend and a new place to stay.

When my friend went to school I broke every rule.
I dug in the dirt where it's wet and cool.

Then I went in the house and made a big mess. I broke things that were important, I guess.

When Mom came home,
boy was I in trouble!
She sent me outside,
"on the double!"
No more time in
the house
and no more soft bed.
Now I lived in the back-
yard by myself instead.

I missed my friend;
he missed me too.
We were unhappy
but what could we do?

A man saw me one day
and took me to stay
in a place I'd be safe
from harm.

The shelter was fine
and helped at the time
but I was lonely and
sad and forlorn.

My luck changed one day when a visitor came whose name I will never forget.

"I'm Dr. David," he said. "I'm an animal Vet and I bet you'll like life on my farm.

You may sleep in my bed. I'll be sure you're well fed and NEVER leave you outside in a storm!"

My new home on the farm is full of fine friends with more animals than you can count on both hands!

Teddy the **DOG** says, "Ruff Ruff y'all!"
He loves his orange ball.
(It's ooey and gooey!)
He's my best friend of all!

RUFF! RUFF!

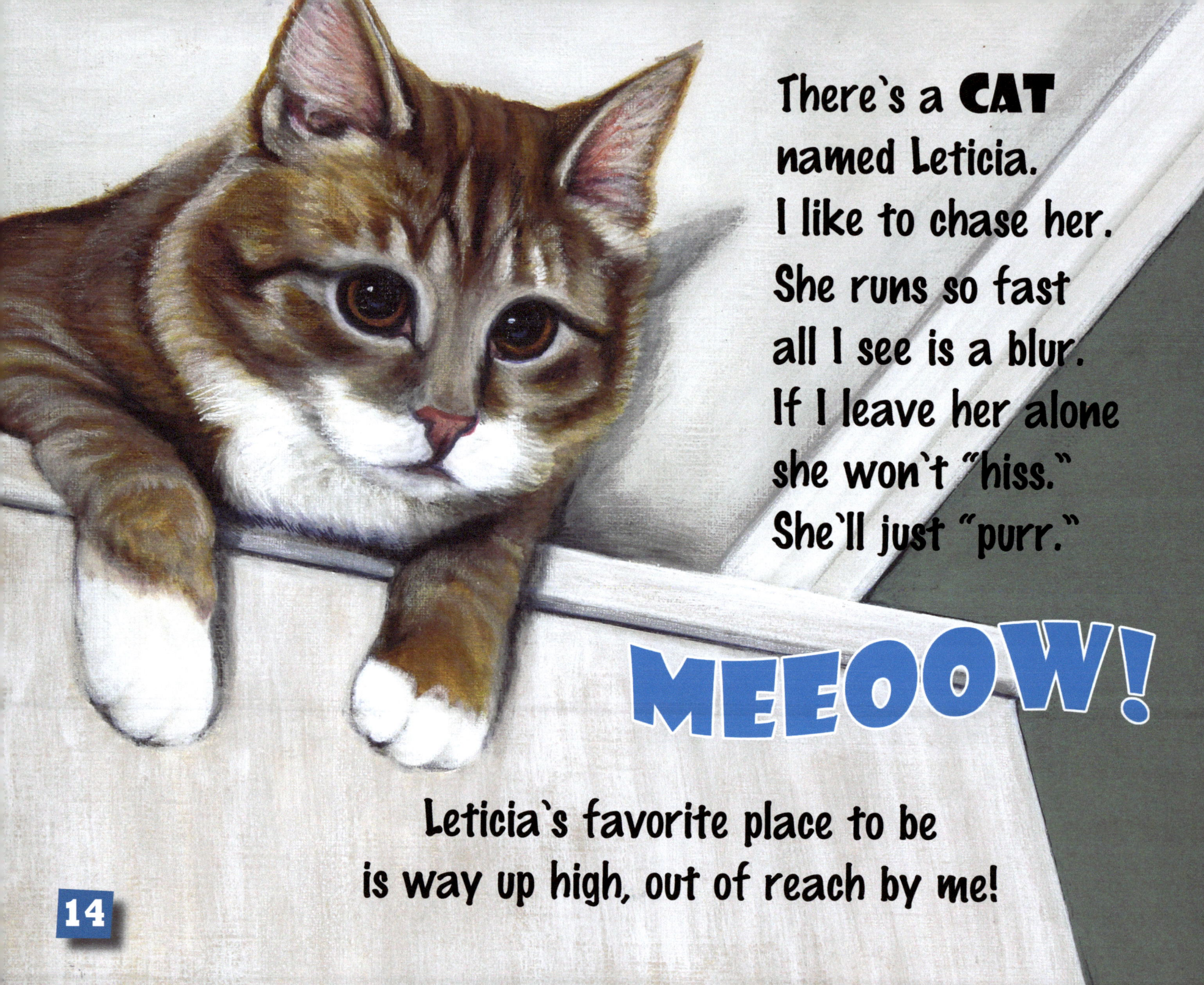

There's a **CAT** name Leticia.
I like to chase her.
She runs so fast
all I see is a blur.
If I leave her alone
she won't "hiss."
She'll just "purr."

MEEOOW!

Leticia's favorite place to be
is way up high, out of reach by me!

They say I should chase **SQUIRRELS** instead, but squirrels run up trees and get too far ahead.

I could sit and wait for a squirrel all day to come down to the ground so that we might play.

But they don't... they just won't... until I go away.

Mavis the **SHEEP** stays in the pasture all day. When she sees me coming, she "Baa Baas" to say, "If you scare my baby you better run for the hills! I won't think that's funny so best you sit still!"

BAA! BAA!

Lucas the **DONKEY** is loud on the farm!
For breakfast and dinner he sounds the alarm.

HEE HAW!

His mouth opens wide;
his eyes shut real tight.
He blasts, "Heehaw, I'm hungry!"
with all of his might!

My friend **CHLOE** has a special job.

She makes milk for us all
and we love her a lot!
Kind, gentle and
pretty too,
Chloe calls out to me
saying, "Moo! Moo!"

MOOO!

Merlin the **GOAT** is a funny guy. He's got a beard and horns and big green eyes.

BLEAT!

I laugh 'til I cry when I see what he eats. When he wants to talk, he sounds off, "Bleat! Bleat!"

COCKADOODLEDOO!

Henry the **ROOSTER** rules the roost. He is the boss in the chicken coop. "Cockadoodledoo!" Henry will say. "Don't bother the hens or the eggs they lay! We've got work to do here. There is no time for play!"

Tom **TURKEY** and Henry get along fine. Tom is a very good friend of mine.

We stay in touch and when I pass by, "Gobble! Gobble!" he'll say. That means "Hi!"

GOBBLE! GOBBLE!

NEIGH! NEIGH!

JEWELL the horse is my prettiest friend.
She has brown and white spots.
Her tail blows in the wind.

Jewell likes carrots.
All horses do.
When we give her a
carrot, she neighs,
"I love you!"

Here on the farm everyday,
my 10 new friends call out and say...

Ruff, Ruff; Oink, Oink; Gobble, Gobble; Bleat, Bleat; Meow; Neigh, Neigh; Baaaaa; Heehaw; Moo, Moo and of course, don't forget... Cockadoodledoo!

Monk the **SKUNK** sleeps all day. He comes out at night when it's too late to play. I don't disturb him because he'll say, "Stay away or else I'll spray."

Rocky and Blossom sleep all day too.

Blossom is a **POSSUM** and Rocky's a **RACCOON**. They're not around when there's work to do.

We catch them in the trash at night when we go to the barn with a **BIG** flashlight!

When the chores are done and the sun starts to set, we go inside to relax and to rest.

It's been a long day. We're both hungry and tired. Dr. David reads a book while we sit by the fire.

At nine o'clock sharp we go to bed where I will have dreams dance in my head of games to be played with my friends at first light.

I SURE AM A LUCKY DOG ALRIGHT!

Toby's Tips

1. Be sure I am always safe and warm.
   Don't leave me outside in a storm!

2. Be sure you remember to feed me well.
   Keep my water bowl full...give me treats...I won't tell!

3. Make sure I have toys to play with so when you're not
   here and I'm home alone, I'll have something to do while
   I wait for you.

4. Don't leave me in the car when it is too hot outside.
   I can't open the doors. I'll be stuck—I might not survive!

5. When it is cool and it's safe for me in the car,
   open the windows to let the air flow
   and leave me some water. I get thirsty you know.

6. Make sure I have a nice soft bed
   on which to sleep and rest my head.
   You know my favorite thing to do is to sleep with you!
   (If that doesn't break a rule!)

7. Take me to the Veterinarian once a year
   for my checkup and vaccinations.
   (You don't like shots and neither do I
   but I'll put up with mine if you're standing nearby!)

8. Give me baths and keep me clean and free of ticks
   and fleas. (Ticks and fleas carry disease
   and if they get on you, they can make you itch too!)

9. Make sure there's a tag on my collar or chip in my fur
   that tells whom to call if I'm lost.
   I can't speak and can't say where I live and this way
   I should make it back home when I'm caught.

10. When we go for a walk keep me safe on a leash
    because if there's a squirrel I might run into the street!

11. Teach me good manners like your mother taught you.
    Don't leave me alone 'til I know all the rules.
    Be kind and don't yell. I have feelings too!

12. Be careful with new dogs or dogs you don't know.
    Stay away from their faces 'til they trust you and so
    don't rush. Take it slow.

13. And if a dog's old and can't see and can't hear,
    be kind and gentle. Be quiet. Stay near.

Please give all of your pets a forever home!

Parent/Teacher CLOSE Reading Guide

(Available for download at Tobyanddrdavid.com)

Step One: Before Reading

Purpose: To establish the background and context for Toby's Story.

Discuss and review background knowledge for animal rescue and farm life:

How do pets get lost?

How do you keep from losing your pet?

What is an animal shelter?

What is the animal adoption process in an animal shelter?

What is a "forever home"?

What is a farm?

Where are farms located?

Have you been to a farm?

How is life on a farm different than life in a city?

Where does the food come from that we buy in a store?

Which animals live on a farm?

Which foods do they provide?

Encourage the telling of personal stories as they relate to pets, pet care, animal rescue and farm animals.

Step Two: Reading the Story

Purpose: To connect the story to real life and develop skills and thought processes as they relate to comprehension.

1. Look at the cover and make predictions.
   Ask: What could this book be about? Who might be Toby?

2. Take a "Picture Walk" through the book. Slowly look at the pictures but do not read the words.
   Ask: Are these illustrations (drawings/paintings) or photographs?
   Which of these animals would live in your house?
   Have you seen any of these animals in real life? Which ones?
   What do you predict this story will be about?

3. Read the first 5 pages. Stop.
   Ask: Why do you think Toby broke every rule?
   If Toby didn't know what the rules were then was it his fault he broke them?
   If someone left food on the plate was it Toby's fault he broke the plate?
   Was it Toby's fault if he was lonely or bored or had no toys or friends to play with?

4. Read pages 6-9. Stop
   Ask: Where is Toby? (answer: ANIMAL shelter)
   What is an ANIMAL shelter? (answer: a place where lost animals are taken) Does Toby look happy there?

5. Read pages 10-11. Stop.
   Ask: What is a Vet? (answer: Vet is "short" for Veterinarian. A Veterinarian is an ANIMAL doctor)
   Do you think Toby will be excited to go with Dr. David?

6. Read pages 12-13. Stop
   Ask: What does Teddy say? (Ruff, Ruff)
   How does Elvis speak? (Oink, Oink)
   What sound does Elvis make when he snorts? When he grunts?

7. Read page 14. Stop.
   Ask: What does it sound like when Leticia hisses?
   When she hisses is she happy or angry?
   What does it mean when Toby says Leticia runs so fast all he sees is a blur?

8. Read page 15. Stop.
   Ask: Have you ever seen a real squirrel? Was it in a tree?
   Is a squirrel a farm animal? Why or why not.

9. Read pages 16-19. Stop.
   Ask: Have you ever heard a donkey "Heehaw"?
   Can you make that sound?
   What crazy things do goats eat? (Everything from paper and cans to clothing...but to stay healthy they eat plants, tree leaves, hay and grain)

10. Read pages 20-21. Stop
   Ask: Why are chickens important farm animals?
   Which day of the year do some call "Turkey Day"?

11. Read pages 22-23. Stop.
   Ask: Have you seen a horse in real life?
   Where was it? Did you ride it?
   Why are horses important animals on a farm?

12. Read page 24. Stop.
   Ask: What happens when a skunk sprays you?
   Is it hard to wash off and get rid of the smell?
   Is the skunk a farm animal? Does he have a job on the farm?
   Can you pet a skunk like you pet a cat?
   What are animals that sleep all day and play all night called? (Nocturnal)

13. Read page 25. Stop
   Ask: Dr. David calls animals that cause trouble "Critters."
   What trouble do Blossom and Rocky cause?
   Are they farm animals or wild animals?

14. Read pages 26-27. Stop.
   Ask: How many people friends did Toby have on the farm?
   (Answer: 2. Dr. David and Emily)
   How many farm animal friends did Toby have?
   (Answer: 10. Teddy, Elvis, Leticia, Mavis, Lucas, Chloe, Merlin, Henry, Tom and Jewell)
   How many Critter friends did Toby have?
   (Answer: 3. Monk, Blossom and Rocky or 4 if you count the squirrel)

Step Three: Extension Activities (after reading)

Purpose: To further incorporate five practices that support early literacy instruction and progression.
(Sing, Talk, Read, Write, Play)

1. Real Life Link: Apply Toby's checklist to the care you give to your own pet.
Make a list of everything you want to remember to do for your pet.

2. Mobile Link: Listen to, clap and sing along with "Old MacDonald Had a Farm."

3. Art Link: Create your own book cover.
Draw your favorite farm animal. What sound does it make?

4. Friend Link: Add a new special friend to your life (person, plant or animal).

5. ESL Link (English as a second language): Learn a word that means "friend" in another language.

6. Fluency Link: Read the story to someone aloud (smooth reading).

7. Writing Link: If the story keeps going, what would happen next?
Add another animal to the farm?
What other things could Dr. David do to show he loves Toby?
What other things could Toby and his friends talk about?

8. Partner Talk Link: Discuss the reasons you like Toby's story with a partner.
What did each of you like best?
Which is your favorite farm animal? Tell each other why this animal is your favorite.

Step Four: Vocabulary Review

Purpose: To define words and expand the application of vocabulary as it relates to telling and understanding Toby's Story.

Page 4 Rules: What is a rule?
Do we have rules in the classroom? Do you have rules at home?
What might be the consequence when a rule is broken?

Page 5 Important: Is there something that means a lot to you?
To your parent? To your teacher?
What makes that something special to you or to someone else?
How might someone feel if something important to them is lost or broken?

Page 6 "on the double": What does this mean?
Has anyone ever asked you to do something "on the double"?
Use "on the double" in a sentence.

Page 8 "thunder and pours": What could this mean?
Do you pour water into a glass?
Is the sky "pouring" water when it rains?

Page 9 Forlorn: Have you ever felt sad?
What does it feel like to be sad?
Use "forlorn" in a sentence.

Page 10 Visitor: What is a visitor?
Have you ever visited someone?
Have you ever visited a dog or cat at an animal shelter?

Page 10 Vet: What is an animal Doctor called? (veterinarian)
What are some words that are "short" for other words?
"Vet" is "short" for Veterinarian. "Doc" is "short" for Doctor.
Do you have a name that is "short" for your name (your "nickname")?

Page 16 "run for the hills": What could this mean?
If you are "running for the hills" should you run fast?
Use "run for the hills" in a sentence.

Page 17 Alarm: What is an alarm?
Why do we have alarms?
Do we have an alarm in the school? What does it sound like?
Are there alarms on clocks? Why?
What do you do when you hear a fire alarm? An alarm clock?

Page 17 "all of his might": What is "might"?
Would you make a sound if you were using all your might to lift something really heavy or throw something a long way?
Use a sentence with "all of my might."

Page 21 "stay in touch":
Do you call your parents to let them know where you are when you are not at home?
Do you keep "in touch" with your parents?
How do you keep "in touch" with your friends when you are not at school?

Page 26 Relax: Does this mean to work or to rest?
Does this mean to slow down and calm down or speed up and get excited?
What do you like to do when you relax?

www.ingramcontent.com/pod-product-compliance
Lightning Source LLC
Chambersburg PA
CBHW042109090526
44591CB00005B/54